THE SEVEN VOYAGES OF SINBAD THE SAILOR

a journey through life

A Play with Music
by
RIC AVERILL

Adapted from the Sir Richard Burton translation of
The 1,001 Arabian Nights

This play is dedicated to my lovely princesses, Jeanne and Trish, who have stayed with me in love and support throughout the many perilous and marvelous voyages of my life, and to my son, Will, who has embarked on a few magnificent odysseys of his own.

THE SEVEN VOYAGES OF SINBAD THE SAILOR was originally produced in 1997 by the Seem-To-Be Players of Lawrence, Kansas, with the following company:

Director . . . . RIC AVERILL
Set Design . . . . MARK REANEY
Costumes and Puppets . . . . JENNIFER GLENN
Music composed and recorded by . . RIC AVERILL
   (Music is dedicated to June and Michael Podgrasi, who have survived a shipwreck and continue to move forward.)

Sinbad the Sailor . . . . KEVIN COMER
Ensemble . . . . KITTY STEFFENS
                              JERRY MITCHELL
                              KASI BROWN

Stage Manager . . . . SAMANTHA KORSHIN

* * * *

Cultural Note

Sinbad is a Merchant Hero, different in many ways from Western folk and mythic heroes. There are clear cross-cultural similarities in some of his adventures, but he is unique, valuing cleverness above all else and being rewarded with wealth. At each of his stages of life, he earns a new name, growing from the most childish, Sinbad the Horseman, to the elder, Sinbad the Ambassador. His demeanor changes as each adventure puts him through a trial and helps him to grow. He may accumulate symbolic costume pieces as well as treasure, adding a necklace, arm braces, a vest, a turban and other trappings of age and wealth throughout the adventure.

THE SEVEN VOYAGES OF SINBAD THE SAILOR

A Play in One Act

Full Cast Of Characters:

SINBAD THE SAILOR, a Persian merchant hero
SINBAD THE PORTER, his namesake, a porter
GUARD #1
GUARD #2
MERCHANT
FIRST MATE
ISLAND MONSTER
STRANGER ON MADAGASCAR
SEA HORSE, later named TIGER
KING OF MADAGASCAR
PEOPLE OF BAGHDAD (actors in costume pieces represent many)
RUKH (a full-size puppet)
BABY RUKH (a small puppet)
SNAKES (hand-held puppets/props)
HIDEOUS ONE-EYED GIANT
HERDER
QUEEN
HORSE
PRINCESS, ugly and annoying
OLD MAN (a marionette)
APES (2)
WOMAN WITH WINGS
RAJAH
GRANDFATHER ELEPHANT
OTHER ELEPHANTS (small puppets, flip targets)

TIME: Long ago.
PLACE: The Seven Seas.

Notes on set, puppetry and costumes at end of script.

Doubling for a Cast of Four:
(The original Seem-To-Be Players production casting)

SINBAD THE SAILOR
ACTOR #1 – SINBAD THE PORTER, ISLAND MONSTER,
           KING OF MADAGASCAR, RUKH,
           HIDEOUS ONE-EYED GIANT, HERDER, HORSE, APE

ACTOR #2 – GUARD #1, MERCHANT, SEA HORSE, PEOPLE OF
           BAGHDAD, BABY RUKH, SNAKES, QUEEN, APE,
           RAJAH

ACTOR #3 – GUARD #2, FIRST MATE, STRANGER ON
           MADAGASCAR, PEOPLE OF BAGHDAD, PRINCESS,
           OLD MAN, WOMAN WITH WINGS, OTHER ELEPHANTS

Doubling for a Cast of Five:

SINBAD THE SAILOR
ACTOR #1 – SINBAD THE PORTER, KING OF MADAGASCAR,
           HIDEOUS ONE-EYED GIANT, HERDER, APE

ACTOR #2 – GUARD #1, MERCHANT, SEAHORSE,
           PEOPLE OF BAGHDAD, BABY RUKH,
           SNAKES, QUEEN, APE, RAJAH

ACTOR #3 – GUARD #2, FIRST MATE, STRANGER ON
           MADAGASCAR, PEOPLE OF BAGHDAD,
           PRINCESS, OLD MAN, WOMAN WITH WINGS,
           OTHER ELEPHANTS

ACTOR #4 – ISLAND MONSTER, PEOPLE OF BAGHDAD, RUKH,
           HORSE, GRANDFATHER ELEPHANT (mostly "puppets")

THE SEVEN VOYAGES OF SINBAD THE SAILOR

SETTING: *A wide backdrop depicting a map of the Persian Gulf and the Indian Ocean is framed by mosaic flats. This storybook-style map illustrates the Seven Voyages of Sinbad the Sailor, showing the locations mentioned in the play, including Baghdad, Persia, Madagascar, India, Borneo, as well as a cartographer's storybook impression of the Rukh, the Monster Island, and the Elephant's Graveyard. R and L of the map are two Persian towers. The map and towers conceal props and costumes which are changed rapidly. Actors enter U between the curtain and the towers, or far R and L around the towers. There are also several wooden unit pieces including two three-dimensional triangles which serve as ramps, two boxes, and several planks to create rafts or tables. These set units are assembled like blocks to represent the various lands that Sinbad visits and will be referred to in the script as "locations" such as "Mountain of the Rukh" or "The Elephant's Graveyard" rather than described in specific detail of construction. In the original production, these geometric building blocks and some fabric were stacked and arranged to create mountains, islands, and caves in much the same manner that a child will create make-believe lands when at play. This method of redefining the space makes it possible to work*

7

on a unit set and create the many environments neces-sary for this epic adventure. In addition, the Arabian ship can be suggested with handheld components, in-cluding a pointed bow, a mast with crow's nest and flag, and a rudder. When these are lifted and moved in a swaying rhythm, the actors seem to be in a sailing ship. To the sides of the set are baskets and chests filled with "treasure."

AT RISE: *Persian music plays as dawning light comes up revealing the map. The two towers and the arrangement of the unit set represent the Inside Court of a Mid-East-ern House. SINBAD THE SAILOR's TWO GUARDS en-ter, sing of an upcoming feast.*

(#1: FEAST MUSIC)

GUARDS.

> **Feast, feast, come to the feast,**
> **The feast of Sinbad the Sailor.**
> **Wealth, food, abundance is yours,**
> **All thanks to Sinbad the Sailor!**

(SINBAD THE PORTER enters carrying a basket, sings of looking for work.)

SINBAD THE PORTER.

> **Work, work, please give me work,**
> **The cry of the poor of Baghdad.**
> **Work, work is all that I need,**
> **The cry of the Porter of Baghdad.**

*(The GUARDS resume singing, as SINBAD THE POR-
TER repeats his verse. The two parts blend. All end up
center, SINBAD THE PORTER between the GUARDS.)*

GUARD #1. Off with you, beggar.

GUARD #2. You heard him. Away with you!

SINBAD THE PORTER. But I'm not a beggar, I'm a porter and I'm looking for work.

GUARD #1. No work here.

GUARD #2. No work for beggars.

SINBAD THE PORTER. But I'm a porter. I carry things
and—

GUARD #1. Not for us you don't.

GUARD #2. Porter or not, you look like a beggar.

GUARD #1. And you act like a fool! So—

*(They get ready to throw him out when SINBAD THE
SAILOR, as an old man, enters. The GUARDS stop and
stand at attention.)*

SINBAD THE SAILOR. What is going on? What is the
commotion, guards?

GUARD #1. A porter, Sinbad, sire.

SINBAD THE PORTER. Sinbad is your name, too? Then,
I'm honored to meet you, sire.

GUARD #2. Then you'll be honored to leave the presence
of my Master.

*(GUARDS again begin to escort SINBAD THE PORTER
off. SINBAD THE SAILOR stops them.)*

SINBAD THE SAILOR. Wait. Your name is Sinbad?

SINBAD THE PORTER. Yes, sir, Sinbad the Porter.

GUARD #1. Arrogance!

GUARD #2. Shall we dispatch him, Master?

SINBAD THE SAILOR. My namesake? Dispatch my namesake? Your name is really Sinbad, my friend?

SINBAD THE PORTER. As truly as truth is true, Master.

SINBAD THE SAILOR. Then it is good fortune that you have come to my house. One must always honor a shared name, Sinbad. You must eat with me.

(He claps his hands and the GUARDS reluctantly sing and bring cornucopias of food to SINBAD THE POR-TER.)

GUARDS.
   Feast, feast, come to the feast,
   The feast of Sinbad the Sailor.

(The GUARDS stand by grimacing.)

SINBAD THE SAILOR. Off, guards. Find somewhere else to make your unpleasant faces.

(The GUARDS grumble, make more ugly faces and exit.)

SINBAD THE SAILOR. My friend, I will tell you my story. For I have sailed the seven seas, I have had seven adventures, and now I find myself seventy-seven years old. I must tell you how I came to be so old, so wise and so very, very rich.

SINBAD THE PORTER *(eating)*. I will listen, as I am your servant.

SINBAD THE SAILOR. When I was but a lad, my father
died and I inherited all his lands and goods. I was rich
and, oh, that money sang out to be spent. I wasted most
of my fortune in two short years on goodies to eat, tricks
and games to play, on ponies and trinkets. So, at the
tender age of seven, I had almost nothing left. My
mother said to me, *(In her voice.)* "Sinbad, you must do
something in the world to save us from misfortune."
SINBAD THE PORTER. So what did you do?
SINBAD THE SAILOR. I took my remaining wealth, pur-
chased trade goods and went to sea with a friendly merchant.

*(Music begins. SINBAD sings as the cast transforms the
set into the Island of the Sea Monster. MERCHANT and
FIRST MATE enter. MERCHANT holds bow of ship and
FIRST MATE holds rudder and mast.)*

(#2: SINBAD SONG, 1ST VOYAGE)

SINBAD THE SAILOR.
   I'm Sinbad the Sailor, a merchant sailor, I.
   Sinbad the Sailor, from coast to coast I fly.
   To adventure, excitement, exploring foreign lands,
   Adventure, excitement, my life in Allah's hands.

(FIRST MATE hands SINBAD the mast.)

MERCHANT & FIRST MATE.
   Sinbad, oh, Sinbad, Where will you go this day?
   The world invites you to sail far away.

SINBAD THE SAILOR *(speaks rhythmically to music and drums). This* is the *story* of my *(beat)* first *voyage.*

MERCHANT. Welcome, Sinbad, to our wonderful ship.

FIRST MATE. Aye. The finest ship that ever sailed the seven seas.

MERCHANT. Load his goods, it's time to sail!

(SINBAD hands MATE a basket of "goods" and they "cast off" and set sail. As SINBAD sings, a MONSTER slinks out and hides under the "Island.")

(#3: TRAVEL WITH TREASURE SONG)

SINBAD THE SAILOR.

I travel with treasures, that fill this mighty boat,
Through storms and through dangers, across the
**   sea we'll float.**
I'm not content, I can't stand still,
I don't know that I ever will.
My restless soul draws me to roam,
The seven seas I call my home.

(Shouting out as they sway back and forth to music and sounds of the ocean.)

SINBAD THE SAILOR. Where do we sail?

MERCHANT. To Basrah! Then to the Indian Ocean. There are trading ports to visit and islands to explore.

FIRST MATE. Aye. We'll chart new ones, you bet.

MERCHANT *(noticing "Island")*. Ahoy! Look yonder! I've not seen that island before.

FIRST MATE. I told you we'd chart new ones, Sinbad, lad. We can give it a name, eh?

SINBAD THE SAILOR. We'll name it Tiger like my pony.

FIRST MATE. Or Paradise, if it's filled with treasure!

(They stop the boat, set parts down.)

MERCHANT. All ashore!

(They move onto the "Island" and look about. A tentacle from the puppet's head slowly peers out. MONSTER punctuates this scene with horrible growling.)

SINBAD THE SAILOR. I don't see anything.

MONSTER. Grrrrrrr.

MERCHANT. Ah, you must be patient. Real treasures can be slow to reveal themselves.

MONSTER. Grrrrrrr.

SINBAD THE SAILOR. But I hear something strange.

MERCHANT. Nonsense, noises of the sea.

SINBAD THE SAILOR *(kneeling down to listen, feeling the surface of the "Island")*. But this island feels strange. More like the back of my pony than dirt on the ground. *(He reaches down, grabs a handful of monster hair.)* Yes, more like hair.

MONSTER *(louder in response to hair pulling. Another tentacle comes out)*. Grrrrrrr.

FIRST MATE. Let's build a fire! I'm hungry.

SINBAD THE SAILOR *(looking at MATE, who pulls out a prop fire and begins to light it)*. I'm not so sure that's a great idea!

MERCHANT. You worry too much, lad. There is nothing on this island. We might as well eat.

(The MONSTER's bulging eyes appear and tentacles begin to sway back and forth.)

MONSTER. Grrrrrrrr.

SINBAD THE SAILOR. You may be right about that. There may be nothing on this island. Because I'm not sure it's an island at all!

MONSTER *(another growl; his whole head emerges).* Grrrrrrrr.

FIRST MATE. Nothing stops me from cooking!

(Lights the fire. There is bright light. The MONSTER growls and screams.)

MONSTER. Aaaargh, murrrrphl, prughulaaargh!

(The "Island" turns over as MONSTER emerges, pushing set pieces about.)

SINBAD THE SAILOR. I was right! It's not an island at all! It's a sea Monster!

MERCHANT. Jump for your lives!

FIRST MATE. Swim to the ship!!!

MONSTER. Aaaaaaaaarrrghghghghghgh!

(They swim, MERCHANT picks up his portion of the ship, exits, yelling back.)

MERCHANT. Swim for you life, Sinbad, swim for your life!

(MONSTER follows FIRST MATE, thwacks and spins MATE around, MATE finally grabs rudder, thwacks MONSTER who howls and scoots off. MATE grabs the mast and exits leaving SINBAD alone, "floating." SINBAD swims about and moves a portion of the set to create Madagascar. He then collapses as though he has just swum ashore.)

(#4: WHY, WHY? SONG)

SINBAD THE SAILOR. This is not what I expected.
(He sings.)
    Why, why, am I left all alone?
    Will this shipwreck be the end of me?
    Why, why, oh, help, hear me moan?
    Why did I ever set out on the sea?

(Shouts.) Hello! Hello!

(A STRANGER sneaks in, hiding behind a "Frond on a Stick," hushes SINBAD.)

STRANGER. Tsk-tsk-tsk-tsk. Quiet, boy! You'll scare them away.
SINBAD THE SAILOR. What?
STRANGER. You'll scare them away.
SINBAD THE SAILOR. Scare who? Who are you?
STRANGER. You are you and you're making too much noise. You'll scare the Seahorses. Hide!

*(Lifts a plank and hands it to SINBAD to hide behind.
SINBAD obeys, but is still confused.)*

SINBAD THE SAILOR. The Seahorse?
STRANGER. Hush! The Seahorse, the Seahorse!

*(STRANGER points as beautiful SEAHORSE enters and
prances about.)*

SINBAD THE SAILOR. I don't see a ... a Seahorse.
STRANGER. Tsk-tsk-tsk!

*(Points. The SEAHORSE approaches them, neighing and
throwing its head back.)*

STRANGER. They are impossible to catch. If they hear
me, or smell you,

(The SEAHORSE starts, noticing them.)

STRANGER. they run and—

*(SINBAD crosses to the SEAHORSE and reaches into his
pouch; clicking his tongue, he holds out a piece of bread.)*

SINBAD THE SAILOR. Here, pony, pony, Seapony. So
pretty, come here, so pretty ... I have a bit of bread left
in my pocket, so soggy but salty and still so good. Come
here, girl. Come here.

*(The SEAHORSE nibbles on the bread and allows SIN-
BAD to pat its head. SINBAD takes a rope from his*

*pouch and uses it as a bridle for the SEAHORSE.
STRANGER is amazed.)*

STRANGER. No one ... no one has ever tamed such a crea-
ture so fast. I must tell the King.

*(STRANGER leaves, calling for KING. Music as SIN-
BAD takes the "reins" and "rides" about.)*

STRANGER. King. King!
SINBAD THE SAILOR. Thatta girl. What a beautiful
horse you are. More precious than jewels or gold.

*(KING enters from opposite side of flat that STRANGER
exited.)*

KING. Yes? What is it?

*(Not seeing anyone, the KING returns behind the Per-
sian flat. STRANGER reenters from the other side.)*

STRANGER. Oh, King? King?

*(STRANGER exits again and KING reenters. Looks
around.)*

KING. Yes?

(STRANGER reenters, shouts.)

STRANGER. King! *(Notices KING, quiets back down.)*
There you are, King. *(Points to SINBAD.)* Just came up

out of the sea on a wooden plank, tamed the Seahorse
outright, he did.

KING. Lad, I say, lad. Who are you?

SINBAD THE SAILOR. Sinbad, Your Majesty. Sinbad the
Horseman. This is my Seapony ... *(Makes up a name on
the spot.)* ... Tiger.

KING. Tiger? Do you suppose Tiger would let me take a
ride?

SINBAD THE SAILOR. I'm sure. Tiger's very friendly.

STRANGER. Your Majesty, be careful, the boy may be a
sorcerer.

KING. Hardly. Come, Tiger. *(SINBAD hands the reins to
the KING, who rides "Tiger" about. KING stops.)* This
is a fine steed, my lad. What would you take for a horse
such as this?

SINBAD THE SAILOR. I shouldn't take anything from
you, Lord. Since you rule this island, the Seahorse is
already yours.

KING. The proper answer, Sinbad the Horseman. For that
answer, I'll give you whatever you wish right now. *(Hands
reins to STRANGER.)*

STRANGER *(grumpily wandering off, leading SEA-
HORSE)*. Why doesn't this ever happen to me?

SINBAD THE SAILOR. Is there a port here, then? Where
merchants come to trade?

KING. Of course.

(They change the set to establish a Port.)

SINBAD THE SAILOR. Then I would like to work here,
and perhaps someday book passage on a ship that will
return me to my own city of Baghdad.

KING. Then you shall work for me until the next ship for Baghdad arrives. And you must convey my best wishes to your Sultan.

SINBAD THE SAILOR. I shall, Your Majesty, and I'm sure he will bless you with more trade.

KING. Good. I wish to have the largest port in the world, able to harbor ships from China, India, Sumatra, Siam—

(MERCHANT enters holding bow of ship as FIRST MATE comes in with mast and rudder.)

MERCHANT. Ahoy, King, what island is this?

KING. Madagascar, my friend. Do you wish to trade here?

MERCHANT. I've finished all my trading. The only goods I have on board belong to a poor fellow who was swallowed by a Sea Monster.

SINBAD THE SAILOR. Wait, Merchant. It's me! Sinbad. I wasn't eaten at all.

KING. You know each other?

MERCHANT. Are you claiming to be Sinbad?

SINBAD THE SAILOR. Remember, I was the one who first suspected the island was not an island at all, but the back of a Monster. *(Tugs on MERCHANT's hair.)* Hairy like my horse... *(MERCHANT growls.)* And growled just like that.

FIRST MATE. Yup, that's him. That's Sinbad.

MERCHANT *(reluctantly agreeing)*. I guess you are. Sinbad, welcome back. We have your goods. *(To FIRST MATE.)* Give him his goods.

(FIRST MATE hands basket to MERCHANT who hands it to SINBAD.)

SINBAD THE SAILOR. And these I will give to the King
of Madagascar. *(Handing the basket to the KING.)* Here
you are, King.

KING *(goes to side of stage and picks up a basket of gems
and pearls).* Ah, and here you are, Sinbad. *(Handing him
treasure.)* My richest necklace of pearls and one hundred
gold coins. You have brought me a most beautiful horse
and for this I am grateful! A blessing on your house always. *(Exits.)*

MERCHANT. Are you ready to return home, Sinbad?

SINBAD THE SAILOR. That I am. *(In rhythm with drums
and music.)* For *that* is the *end* of my *(beat)* first *voyage*!

*(MERCHANT and MATE exit with ship. SINBAD THE
PORTER enters and sits by SINBAD THE SAILOR. The
TWO GUARDS reenter and begin the set change to represent the Island of the Giant Bird, complete with flowers and diamonds. This change will be completed as
characters enter and exit over the next few lines.)*

SINBAD THE SAILOR. So, Sinbad the Porter. Come to
my house tomorrow night and I will tell you of my second voyage.

SINBAD THE PORTER. I will, that I will.

*(Transition music as PORTER walks to side of stage,
"sleeps," then comes back toward SINBAD THE SAILOR.
GUARD #1 stops him.)*

GUARD #1. Halt! Who are you that dares to approach the
house of Sinbad the Sailor?

SINBAD THE PORTER. I'm Sinbad the Porter and *I* was invited.

GUARD #1 *(grumbles)*. Oh, yes, I remember, well, go ahead.

(GUARD exits. SINBAD THE SAILOR hands SINBAD THE PORTER an apple and renews his story.)

SINBAD THE SAILOR. Ah, Sinbad.

SINBAD THE PORTER. Yes, Sinbad?

SINBAD THE SAILOR. It is good luck to have my namesake return.

SINBAD THE PORTER. My pleasure, I assure you.

SINBAD THE SAILOR. I will now tell you the story of my return to sea. *(PORTER sits and begins to eat.)* I was so thankful to Allah that I returned safely with the gold and pearls that I rewarded all who came to welcome me home.

("PEOPLE" enter and line up. These are actors who take turns being a "line" of different people, changing characters using scarves as headpieces, skirts, veils, etc. They grumble thanks as SINBAD THE SAILOR hands them gold pieces and pearls from the KING's treasure basket.)

SINBAD THE SAILOR. One for you. Thank you for visiting, Grandmama. Here you are, Doctor. Wonderful to see you, Scherezade. Greetings to you as well, Blacksmith. Yes and for you, and you, and you, and you, and you...

("PEOPLE" exit.)

SINBAD THE PORTER. Gracious, you had many friends.

SINBAD THE SAILOR. A wealthy man has more friends than fingers and toes, and a poor man is lucky to have his own thumbs.

(MERCHANT and FIRST MATE enter with boat.)

SINBAD THE SAILOR. Soon I was left with only the pearls. So the need for money and the desire for adventure sent me, a very young seventeen-year-old, into the world once more!

(He joins the MERCHANT and FIRST MATE, all moving with the music, "in the boat.")

(#5: SINBAD SONG, 2ND VOYAGE)

SINBAD THE SAILOR.
   **I'm Sinbad the Sailor, a merchant sailor, I ...
   Sinbad the Sailor, from coast to coast I fly.
   To adventure, excitement, exploring foreign lands,
   Adventure, excitement, my life in Allah's hands.**

ALL.
   **Sinbad, oh, Sinbad, Where will you go this day?
   The world invites you, to sail far away.**

SINBAD THE SAILOR *(stops singing and speaks rhythmically). This* is the *story* of my *(beat)* second *voyage.*

MERCHANT. Welcome, Sinbad, you will join us again?

FIRST MATE. Aye. Wasn't such good luck having you aboard last time. I was almost eaten alive.

MERCHANT. Never mind that, mate, he's got money and it's time to sail!

(#6: TREASURE REPRISE)

SINBAD THE SAILOR (sings again).
I travel with treasures, that fill this mighty boat,
Through storms and through dangers, across the
sea we'll float.

SINBAD THE SAILOR (shouting out as they sway back and forth). Where do we sail?

MERCHANT. Directly to the Indian Ocean. Then on to Ceylon at the tip of India.

FIRST MATE. Aye. If we don't have the misfortune you brought on us the last time.

MERCHANT. Quit complaining, mate. Look yonder! I've not seen that island before.

FIRST MATE. Eh? It's not a monster now, is it?

SINBAD THE SAILOR. No, there are trees and beautiful flowers and something sparkling high up on the mountainside.

FIRST MATE. Sparkling, you say? Sparkling? Aye. Like diamonds. We should land, Captain, and look about.

MERCHANT. So we will. But we can only stay for one hour—

FIRST MATE (repeating each command with an air of authority, almost interrupting). One hour.

MERCHANT. If you aren't back—

FIRST MATE. Be back.

MERCHANT. By the time the sun drops behind the mount—

FIRST MATE. By the time the... *(MERCHANT growls at FIRST MATE to stop repetition. MATE quickly abbreviates.)* ...Sunset.

MERCHANT. Sunset! The ship leaves without you.

(They walk about on the island. They each pick a flower and smell it.)

MERCHANT. What a beautiful smell. Reminds me of my home in Persia, where as a small boy... *(He drifts off to sleep and falls to ground.)*

FIRST MATE. I'm going to look for those sparkling... *(Also drifts off, slipping into slumber.)*

SINBAD THE SAILOR. These flower are so beautiful. But look, the others are falling... The flowers make you... *(He falls away from the other two, nearly out of sight.)* ...sleepy. *(He sleeps. Music.)*

(Lights dim. MERCHANT wakes up suddenly.)

MERCHANT. What? The sun! Look, the sun! It's slipped behind the mountains. Mate, Sinbad! We must leave or be caught by the winds tonight.

FIRST MATE *(also waking)*. Huh? What happened? I didn't find the sparkling diamonds.

MERCHANT. Never mind that. Where's Sinbad? *(They look briefly.)*

FIRST MATE. I don't see him. It's getting dark.

MERCHANT. He was warned. Let's go!

(They get in boat and leave "Island," swaying to boat music. SINBAD awakens, groggy.)

SINBAD THE SAILOR. Oh, no more flowers for me. But just in case... *(He grabs a flower, holds his nose and puts it in his pouch. Walks to where the ship docked.)* ...where is the ship? *(Looks at sky, mountain then sea.)* They've left without me. I slept so long. I wish I had never left Baghdad. *(There is a frightening screech. SIN-BAD looks about.)* What was that? *(Another screech.)* How odd. I should be terribly frightened but it is only a distant screech. *(Another screech, but louder and closer.)* Maybe not so distant. But still, that shouldn't scare me.

(A puppet SNAKE slithers out from Under the Mountain near him and hisses.)

SINBAD THE SAILOR. A snake! Now that should scare me.

(The loudest screech yet as RUKH, a giant bird, enters.)

SINBAD THE SAILOR. That does scare me!

(SINBAD hides as the RUKH sweeps down and picks up the SNAKE and flies around the stage and toward the Mountain, dropping the SNAKE into a nest that appears on the mountaintop. The BIRD flies off.)

SINBAD THE SAILOR. It's taking the snake way up into the mountains where the sparkling... sparkling... diamonds?

(Another SNAKE pokes its head out. SINBAD looks at it, takes a flower from his pouch.)

SINBAD THE SAILOR. You are not a snake. You are bait. *(SNAKE hisses and squirms.)* You like flowers, little snake? *(SINBAD holds the flower to SNAKE's nose. It suddenly flops still. SINBAD grabs it and holds it up in the air.)* Here, birdy, come here!

(There is another screech as the RUKH reappears and swoops toward the SNAKE in SINBAD's hand. SINBAD is taken for a ride. As they approach the Mountain nest, an egg appears in it. The entire area is surrounded by diamonds. SINBAD gasps as RUKH drops both the SNAKE and SINBAD into the nest and flies off.)

SINBAD THE SAILOR. Diamonds. Hundreds of diamonds. The sad thing is that I'm over five thousand feet up in the air. Hmmmm...

(He stuffs diamonds into his pockets. There is a cracking sound. He looks around. More cracking. Suddenly the egg splits and a tiny hand puppet BABY RUKH emerges and starts squeaking and squawking.)

SINBAD THE SAILOR. Shhh. Your Mommy will come home and kill me. Cute birdy. *(Pets it. The BABY BIRD bites him.)* Not so cute birdy. Shhhhh. Here have a little snake.

(He holds up a little SNAKE and the BABY BIRD eats it. Loud screeching as RUKH enters again. SINBAD crouches and starts flapping his arms and squawking like the BABY BIRD.)

SINBAD THE SAILOR. Hello, Momma Rukh, you had twins this time, see? Squawk! Squawk!

(The big RUKH flies above them, smelling and peering at them curiously, realizes there is a stranger in the nest and flies backward, ready to charge. RUKH makes huge sound and charges. Just in time, SINBAD holds up his extra flower.)

SINBAD THE SAILOR. A flower, Momma Rukh?

(The RUKH smells it and flops over the nest, almost squashing the BABY BIRD who squawks. SINBAD pulls off his belt and ties it to the foot of the RUKH. The RUKH wakes up, looks about, then flies off, dragging SINBAD with him. As they fly, the STRANGER walks across, looking up.)

STRANGER. My, who is that up in the sky tied to that Rukh?

SINBAD THE SAILOR. It is I, Sinbad the Adventurer. *(He lets this last word trail off as he lets go and tumbles toward his home.)*

STRANGER. Let it be known! Sinbad has flown!

(STRANGER exits as SINBAD lands at the foot of entering GUARD #1.)

GUARD #1. Sinbad, sire? Is that you? Where have you been?

SINBAD THE SAILOR. Never mind, just allow me to say that I'm glad I could drop back in here at home. *(Then*

rhythmically.) And *that* is the *end* of my *(beat)* second
voyage!

*(SINBAD THE PORTER enters and sits by SINBAD.
THE SAILOR.)*

SINBAD THE PORTER. Another enchanting tale, sire.
SINBAD THE SAILOR. Thank you for listening, Sinbad
the Porter. Tomorrow night I will tell you of my third
voyage.
SINBAD THE PORTER. Until tomorrow.

*(Transition music as PORTER walks to side of stage,
sleeps, then comes back to "House." GUARD #1 moves
to stand in his way.)*

GUARD #1. Halt! *(Looks at PORTER, PORTER looks
back, smiles. GUARD #1 grumbles and steps out of his
way.)* Never mind.

*(GUARD #1 exits, very grumpy. PORTER approaches
SINBAD.)*

SINBAD THE SAILOR. Sinbad.
SINBAD THE PORTER. Sinbad.
SINBAD THE SAILOR. Are you ready once again?
SINBAD THE PORTER. Of course, sire.

*(They move the set to represent the cave on the Island of
the Hideous Giant.)*

SINBAD THE SAILOR. I lived well on the diamonds for many years. But when I turned twenty-seven I became restless. I'd had good fortune but wanted more. So, without thought for my mother or my city of Baghdad, I sold the diamonds for trade goods and once more set out for sea.

(The MERCHANT and FIRST MATE enter with boat.)

(#7: SINBAD SONG, 3RD VOYAGE)

MERCHANT & FIRST MATE *(singing).*
Sinbad, oh, Sinbad, Where will you go this day?
The world invites you, to sail far away.

SINBAD THE SAILOR *(with music and drum). This* is the *story* of my *(beat)* third *voyage.*
MERCHANT. Oh, Sinbad? You are in Baghdad?
FIRST MATE. Aye, we thought you were dead.
SINBAD THE SAILOR. You left me for dead on the Island of Diamonds.
FIRST MATE. Diamonds, sparkling diamonds. Drats. I knew I should have stayed there. Easy pickings.
SINBAD THE SAILOR. The Island of Diamonds, snakes and giant birds.
FIRST MATE. The Rukh? You saw the giant Rukh?
SINBAD THE SAILOR. I rode the giant Rukh.
MERCHANT. And lived? We are honored, Sinbad the Adventurer, to have you aboard.
SINBAD THE SAILOR. Where are we going?
MERCHANT. To the Island of the Apes, near Borneo, to trade for coconuts.

SINBAD THE SAILOR. Then let's set sail!
MERCHANT. Indeed! We're off!

(#8: TREASURE REPRISE)

SINBAD THE SAILOR *(sings)*.
I travel with treasures, that fill this mighty boat,
Through storms and through dangers, across the
sea we'll float.

MERCHANT. Ah, out of the Persian Gulf we sail, into the
Indian Ocean. Then on to the coast of Borneo.
FIRST MATE. Aye. Surely we'll make it this time without
any misfortune from you. *(There is chaotic music and
wild lighting as a storm builds and brews.)* I've spoken
too soon again!
MERCHANT. It's a typhoon! Hold on for your lives!
FIRST MATE. We'll be shipwrecked for sure!
SINBAD THE SAILOR. The sails, lower the sails!

*(They struggle. Lights go crazy, then there is a crashing
sound. They are shipwrecked.)*

FIRST MATE. We've landed, like it or not.
MERCHANT. The ship. It's ruined. *(They both look at
SINBAD.)* What have you brought upon us?
SINBAD THE SAILOR. It's not my fault.

*(They both huff and look around island. Suddenly a huge
booming noise is heard. They look up.)*

MERCHANT. Now what?

FIRST MATE. We are all going to die.

SINBAD THE SAILOR. Come, hide behind these rocks. Don't just stand there quivering and quaking.

(SINBAD grabs FIRST MATE who follows him and MERCHANT into hiding. Then, from backstage comes a HIDEOUS GIANT, who has but one eye.)

HIDEOUS GIANT. Urrrrrrgh. What do I smell? So near my cave what do I smell?

FIRST MATE. We *are* all going to die.

SINBAD THE SAILOR. Shhh.

HIDEOUS GIANT. Unnnnnnngh. What do I hear?! So near my cave what do I hear?

MERCHANT *(yells in nervousness)*. Nothing!

SINBAD THE SAILOR. I don't think he'll believe you.

(HIDEOUS GIANT moves quickly to the rocks and pulls the MERCHANT out, then reaches in and pulls the FIRST MATE out, then SINBAD and shoves them all into his Cave.)

HIDEOUS GIANT. Aaaaaahhhhh. My dinner. One, two, three. Dinner for three days. *(He pinches and pokes at them.)*

SINBAD THE SAILOR. Don't grab me. I won't be tender to eat if you're all the time pinching me.

HIDEOUS GIANT. Huh? Who are you?

SINBAD THE SAILOR. Sinbad the Hero. That's who I am.

HIDEOUS GIANT. Hero. Hero sandwich! Hee-hee-hee. I'll roast you, one each day.

(MERCHANT and FIRST MATE whimper.)

FIRST MATE. I told you we're dead.

MERCHANT. Sinbad, what shall we do?

HIDEOUS GIANT. Don't talk. I don't like talking food. *(Looks at them.)* Which human I eat first? *(Pokes and prods the MERCHANT.)* Ah, tasty. *(Prods FIRST MATE.)* Ah, shivery and shaky. *(Moves toward SIN-BAD.)* Ah...

SINBAD THE SAILOR *(steps forward, refusing to be prodded)*. Me. You should eat me first.

HIDEOUS GIANT. Huh? No one ever volunteered before.

SINBAD THE SAILOR. I must tell you, though, I'm best cooked in a very hot fire. Lots and lots of coals.

HIDEOUS GIANT. Lots of coals?

SINBAD THE SAILOR. Yes. Burn the fire down so there are many ashes. That's the best way to cook me.

HIDEOUS GIANT. How you know this?

SINBAD THE SAILOR. It's an old family recipe.

HIDEOUS GIANT. Hmmmmmm. You three sit. I burn down to ashes. *(They stand, shaking.)* Sit!

(They sit quickly. HIDEOUS GIANT works on fire as others whisper.)

MERCHANT. What are we to do once he's eaten you?

SINBAD THE SAILOR. He won't eat me.

FIRST MATE. Look, just beyond the fire pit. Treasure. Silver.

SINBAD THE SAILOR. Shh.

HIDEOUS GIANT. Where the human I eat first? Fire ready.

SINBAD THE SAILOR. Here I am, Hideous Giant. But your fire isn't quite ready.

HIDEOUS GIANT. It's not?

SINBAD THE SAILOR. No. You need to blow on the coals and scatter the ashes. Then roast me on the fire!

HIDEOUS GIANT. You sure?

SINBAD THE SAILOR. Of course.

HIDEOUS GIANT. Blow on coals. *(He leans forward. He blows, a huge wind sound as ashes fly up in his face.)* Ashes! Ashes in my eye!

(He stands, holding his hands over his eye. SINBAD runs to him and gives him a shove so that he falls and lands on his bottom in the fire. He jumps up, grabs his behind, screams and runs off.)

HIDEOUS GIANT. Fire! Fire! Help!!

SINBAD THE SAILOR. Stuff your pockets with treasure and let's go!

(They grab treasure, shoving it in their pockets and mouths, then run out of the cave to the ship.)

MERCHANT. Very good. Have you forgotten! The ship is broken up.

SINBAD THE SAILOR. Then grab a snake! Quickly! Grab a snake!! Hold it in the air!

(They look at him like he is crazy.)

MERCHANT. Are you crazy?

(SINBAD grabs three SNAKES, tosses two to them, then holds his up in the air.)

FIRST MATE. I'm not going to grab a snake! I'm not, I'm not, I'm not!

(The RUKH comes flying across and snaps up SINBAD's SNAKE, swooping him off. As he flies off, the MERCHANT and FIRST MATE grab their SNAKES and wave them in the air, following SINBAD.)

FIRST MATE & MERCHANT. Wait for us! Wait for us!!

(SINBAD "falls" back on stage, at his home.)

SINBAD THE SAILOR *(rhythmically)*. *That* is the *end* of my *(beat)* third *voyage*! *(Then, speaking again.)* But by the age of thirty seven, I grew lonely. Even with my family around me and all my friends. Even with my wealth. So once again, I decided to set out to sea.

(The MERCHANT and FIRST MATE enter with the boat.)

(#9: SINBAD SONG, 4TH VOYAGE)

MERCHANT & FIRST MATE *(singing)*.
    Sinbad, oh, Sinbad, say it once again!

SINBAD THE SAILOR *(rhythmically)*. *This* is the *story* of my *(beat)* fourth *voyage*.
MERCHANT. Sinbad? Please, wouldn't you like to take your cargo aboard another ship?

FIRST MATE. Aye. Every time you sail with us we end up
    shipwrecked or near eaten.
SINBAD THE SAILOR. Haven't you always returned to
    Baghdad with treasure?
MERCHANT. I suppose ...
FIRST MATE. If you want to be particular.
SINBAD THE SAILOR. Then what harm can come of
    traveling with me *this* time?

(They consider this for a moment, nod their heads. Sud-
denly there is a huge howling wind sound.)

MERCHANT. Another typhoon! He's done it again!
FIRST MATE. Cast off the troublemaker! It's his fault.
MERCHANT. Too late. We'll all be cast off!

(A storm overtakes them and they are swept "off the boat."
As they "shipwreck" they set up the Island of the Queen.
They land, panting. HERDER enters in robe with tray of
fruit. He is very slimy.)

HERDER. Ah, my friends, shipwrecked?
SINBAD THE SAILOR. Yes, we are.
MERCHANT *(pointing to SINBAD)*. It happens every time
    we travel with *him*.
FIRST MATE. Aye. But we usually end up with treasure.
    Do you have any?
SINBAD THE SAILOR. Who are you?
HERDER. I am a Herder, looking for strays to add to my
    flock.
SINBAD THE SAILOR *(suspicious)*. What do you herd?

HERDER. So many questions, when you have just survived
the terrible storm. Here, eat some of this fine fruit; stops
the scurvy, feeds the hungry, makes fine men and
women finer still.

MERCHANT. Finer than I already am? Wonderful. *(He
grabs some fruit and eats it. FIRST MATE does as well.)*
That's delicious.

FIRST MATE. Sinbad, eat some of this. Aye, this fruit
may be the treasure of this island.

SINBAD THE SAILOR. Nothing is given away for free.
What do you want of us, Herder?

HERDER. I want you to stay with us. Join us. This is the
finest island you will ever land on.

FIRST MATE. This is the finest fruit I've ever landed on.

MERCHANT. We must have more of this. We should trade
with you. *(He becomes hypnotized and trails off his last
few words.)* What will you take for bushels of this ...

HERDER. Not a single gold piece, my friend, not a jewel,
not a pearl. The island is full of this fruit and I simply
give it to whoever lands on our shore. *(MERCHANT and
FIRST MATE are eating methodically, both now hypnotized.)* Isn't it fine?

MERCHANT. Isn't it fine?

FIRST MATE. Isn't it fine?

HERDER *(to SINBAD)*. And you, sir?

MERCHANT. You, sir?

FIRST MATE. You, sir?

SINBAD THE SAILOR *(looks at them, then at HERDER)*.
It is free, you say?

HERDER. It is free.

MERCHANT. It is free.

FIRST MATE. It is free.

SINBAD THE SAILOR. How free can it be when these
two are dumbstruck, repeating everything you say? Ex-
actly what do you herd? And who are you?

HERDER. Too many questions.

MERCHANT. Too many.

FIRST MATE. Questions.

HERDER. This way, my friends. We'll leave this curious
one behind.

SINBAD THE SAILOR. You expect me to leave without
my shipmates?

HERDER. They don't want you.

*(Throws fruit at SINBAD. The others mimic him and
throw fruit on their lines as well.)*

FIRST MATE. We don't want you.

MERCHANT. We don't want you.

SINBAD THE SAILOR *(takes cover)*. Fools! He's fed you
the "following fruit." You're hypnotized!

HERDER. Come with me, my shipwrecked friends. *(Exits,
leading them off.)* Come join the herd with me. You belong to the Queen.

MERCHANT. We belong to the Queen.

FIRST MATE. We belong to the Queen.

SINBAD THE SAILOR *(watches them go)*. I don't belong
to the Queen and I need to find some way off this island.

(QUEEN enters, riding a strong HORSE, bareback.)

QUEEN. Whoa! *(She stops her HORSE.)* Who are you,
man? What are you doing away from the herd?

SINBAD THE SAILOR. I'm Sinbad the Hero, Your Majesty.

QUEEN. And why aren't you working in the mines with the others?

SINBAD THE SAILOR. I didn't eat the "following" food. I work only for myself and Allah.

QUEEN. But there are diamonds and rubies and emeralds to be dug and presented to me, the Queen.

SINBAD THE SAILOR *(looks at her and the HORSE disdainfully)*. I would hardly think that a queen who rides bareback would be worthy of such jewels.

QUEEN. I beg your pardon. In two seconds I could have my guards here to chop off your head.

SINBAD THE SAILOR. If they don't fall off their horses.

QUEEN. What are you talking about?

SINBAD THE SAILOR. Have you never heard of a saddle, Your Majesty?

QUEEN. Saddle? *(SINBAD pulls "leather" from his bag and "stitches" it together.)* What are you doing, lad? What is that hideous contraption?

SINBAD THE SAILOR *(finishes a makeshift saddle, places it on the reluctant HORSE)*. Now, get on your horse and see if he doesn't ride better!

QUEEN. I've never heard of such a thing. Ride upon a cushion? *(She hops on and "rides." She enjoys it.)* My, this is wondrous thing. Where do you come from, that they make such wonderful things?

SINBAD THE SAILOR. Baghdad, Your Majesty, in Persia. Where the finest saddle makers are treated like princes, and the Queens never ride bareback.

QUEEN. Ah, then you, too, shall live in majesty, Sinbad the Hero. You will be part of my royal court, make saddles, and I will let you marry the beautiful princess, my daughter.

SINBAD THE SAILOR. More than I had planned for. I've never been married.

(PRINCESS enters. She has long, braided hair that stands nearly straight up. She is definitely ugly, bordering on goofy.)

PRINCESS. Hello, hello, hello.

SINBAD THE SAILOR *(surprised and a little distressed)*. Oh, my!

QUEEN. Here is your princess, Sinbad the Husband.

SINBAD THE SAILOR. I could not marry her.

PRINCESS. Sure you could, sweetie.

SINBAD THE SAILOR. I couldn't.

PRINCESS. Sure you could!

SINBAD THE SAILOR. I couldn't.

PRINCESS. You could.

SINBAD THE SAILOR. I couldn't.

PRINCESS. You could.

SINBAD THE SAILOR. I...

QUEEN *(steps forward and grabbing him by the ear)*. You can and you will! And you'll be happy, unless you want to go to the mines with your shipwrecked friends.

SINBAD THE SAILOR. Then let us be married.

PRINCESS. Ahhh. Yes, oh, yes, oh, yes, oh, yes.

(PRINCESS drags him off. QUEEN "rides" the HORSE in a circle, music signals time passing. QUEEN dismounts, HORSE exits.)

QUEEN. Sinbad. Sinbad. More saddles!

(SINBAD enters, carrying more saddles, weary.)

SINBAD THE SAILOR. There, is that enough?

QUEEN. Yes, we now have more saddles than horses! And here are emeralds, rubies and sapphires for your personal treasury. And the armbands of royalty.

(SINBAD puts treasure in his pouch. PRINCESS staggers on and dies.)

PRINCESS. Husband. I ... ugh ... pllllll!

SINBAD THE SAILOR. My wife has been sick.

QUEEN *(leans down and lifts PRINCESS' limp arm, drops it)*. Sick? She's dead. Died of a fever. Such a beautiful girl.

SINBAD THE SAILOR. I'll ... I'll ... miss her. Somewhat.

QUEEN. No, you won't. You'll be with her.

SINBAD THE SAILOR. Excuse me?

QUEEN. It's our custom. When a husband loses a wife or a wife loses a husband, the remaining spouse is thrown into the burial cave with the one they lose. That way you can be together for eternity.

(The dead PRINCESS sits up and puckers her lips.)

PRINCESS. Kiss, kiss, kiss, kiss, kiss ...

SINBAD THE SAILOR *(pushes her back down)*. You're dead. *(To QUEEN.)* I am to be thrown in a cave with her forever?

PRINCESS *(repeat performance)*. Kiss, kiss, kiss, kiss, kiss ...

QUEEN *(pushes her down)*. Honey, you are dead.

PRINCESS. Oh, sorry, Mother.

SINBAD THE SAILOR. I'm *not* going to be thrown in a cave with her. I'm from Baghdad, and we don't have this custom in Persia. Who will make your saddles for you?

QUEEN. I can teach others. And you can take your treasure with you to Paradise. Herder!

(HERDER enters with fruit.)

QUEEN. Drag my sweet daughter to her tomb and throw him in with her.

HERDER. Yes, Your Majesty.

(SINBAD turns to escape but HERDER stuffs a piece of fruit in his mouth.)

SINBAD THE SAILOR. But I...

HERDER. Follow me. *(He starts to drag the PRINCESS. She's heavy.)*

SINBAD THE SAILOR *(hypnotized)*. Follow you.

HERDER. Help me carry her.

SINBAD THE SAILOR. Help you carry her.

(As they carry her, PRINCESS opens eyes.)

PRINCESS. Kiss, kiss, kiss, kiss, kiss...

HERDER & SINBAD THE SAILOR. You're dead!

PRINCESS. Oh, yeah, every time I have to remember, "Pretty Princess, you're dead."

(They lay her out ceremoniously. Music becomes low and ominous. SINBAD is lured by the HERDER, laid out in a similar ceremonial burial position. HERDER exits.)

SINBAD THE SAILOR. To face death at the young age of thirty-seven. Sinbad the Husband becomes Sinbad the Dead Man.

(There is the sound of picks chipping. PRINCESS slips offstage.)

SINBAD THE SAILOR. What's that? *(More sounds of tapping and hammering.)* Someone else is under the earth with me. Hello?
MERCHANT *(from behind the set a voice is heard)*. Hello?
SINBAD THE SAILOR. Who is there?
MERCHANT *(pokes head out).* The Merchant of Baghdad.
SINBAD THE SAILOR. You're alive? It's Sinbad here!
MERCHANT. Sinbad?

(MERCHANT disappears. There is the sound of voices talking. MERCHANT and FIRST MATE poke their heads out and look at SINBAD, then duck their heads back in and discuss some more, come to a decision, then poke heads back out to talk to SINBAD.)

MERCHANT. We're going to try to escape a different direction.
FIRST MATE. Completely different from yours.
MERCHANT. Goodbye.
SINBAD THE SAILOR. Wait! I have precious gems; rubies, emeralds and sapphires.

(There is a loud crash and FIRST MATE enters, followed by MERCHANT.)

FIRST MATE. Treasure?

(SINBAD fills their hands with precious gems.)

MERCHANT. With you there is always treasure. There's always trouble as well.

FIRST MATE. Aye, but treasure is worth all the trouble.

SINBAD THE SAILOR. Give me one of your picks, and we'll tunnel our way out of here.

(MATE gives SINBAD a pick. MERCHANT gives MATE a pick. They "tunnel off," working their way backstage. Music starts up and they sing, also changing the unit set for The Mountain of the Apes.)

(#10: SINBAD SONG, END OF 4TH VOYAGE)

SINBAD THE SAILOR, MERCHANT & FIRST MATE.
  **Adventure, Excitement, Let's leave this foreign land,
  Adventure, Excitement, Our lives in Allah's hands.**

  **Sinbad, oh, Sinbad, Once more you've made it home!
  Sinbad, please stay there, and say you'll never roam.
  We come home with treasures, That fill a mighty
    boat,
  From shipwreck to riches, Across the sea we float.**

(MERCHANT and FIRST MATE move to the side of the stage, picking up the boat for the fifth voyage.)

SINBAD THE SAILOR *(rhythmically). That* was the *story* of my *(beat)* fourth *voyage. (Speaking again.)* Yet, by the time I was forty-seven, I looked for a ship that would take me across the seas to India, a country I had never explored. *(Rhythmically.)* So *this* is the *story* of my *(beat)* fifth *voyage!*

(See #13: SINBAD CHANT, 5TH-7TH VOYAGES)

SINBAD THE SAILOR. Merchant? Oh, Merchant?

(The MERCHANT and FIRST MATE enter, see SINBAD, turn and start off.)

MERCHANT. No, no, no, no, no, no, no.

FIRST MATE. We're not getting in another boat with you. No way.

MERCHANT. No, no, no, no, no, no, no.

SINBAD THE SAILOR *(holds up a bag of gold).* Gold? Ten thousand pieces of gold?

FIRST MATE. Uh...on second thought... *(Looks at MERCHANT, then together.)*

MERCHANT & FIRST MATE. Yes, yes, yes, yes, yes, yes, yes.

MERCHANT. But *you* have to hide.

FIRST MATE. We're going to cover you with a blanket so the gods of the storm and monsters and misadventures won't even know you're aboard.

SINBAD THE SAILOR. But, I'll suffocate.

MERCHANT. No, you won't. *(Throws a blanket over SINBAD, looks around.)* Set sail! Uh, Sinbad is not with us!

FIRST MATE. Whoever might be listening? We do *not* know Sinbad. He is definitely not aboard.

MERCHANT. Never heard of him. Haven't seen him.

(The RUKH sneaks on behind them. Suddenly screeches, flies back to charge.)

MERCHANT & FIRST MATE. The Rukh!

FIRST MATE. This is all your fault.

MERCHANT. Overboard you go!

(They toss the bundled SINBAD overboard)

FIRST MATE. We'll never sail with you again! *(The RUKH swoops back down upon them.)* Run for your lives!

MERCHANT. Swim for it!

(They leave the boat and swim off, pursued by the RUKH. SINBAD pulls the blanket off and struggles to "shore." He sings.)

(#11: WHY, WHY? SONG)

SINBAD THE SAILOR.
> **Why, why, am I left all alone?**
> **Will this shipwreck be the end of me?**
> **Why, why, oh, help, hear me moan?**
> **Why did I ever set out on the sea?**

(Speaks.) Now, what part of the world am I in?

(An OLD MAN enters, walking toward him. The OLD MAN is a bizarre, wrinkly puppet with spindly, attached arms and legs, manipulated by one of the actors clothed in black.)

SINBAD THE SAILOR. Old Man? What are you doing here?

OLD MAN *(in a strange voice).* I wish to cross that stream.

SINBAD THE SAILOR. Why don't you?

OLD MAN. I am old. I need someone to carry me across the stream on their back.

SINBAD THE SAILOR. I hope someone will.

OLD MAN. I was thinking *you* might carry me.

SINBAD THE SAILOR. Since you are so very old, I will carry you. But then I must make my way back to Baghdad.

OLD MAN. Fine. *(SINBAD lifts the OLD MAN onto his shoulders.)* Very nice. Very comfortable, lad.

SINBAD THE SAILOR. For you. Here we go. *(They "cross" the stream on the "Mountain of the Apes.")* Now, I'll put you down.

OLD MAN. I don't think so.

SINBAD THE SAILOR. What did you say?

OLD MAN. You can't put me down. Your new job shall be to carry me around forever.

SINBAD THE SAILOR. I'm sorry, but I've never stayed at a job that long. *(Tries to get the OLD MAN off his back.)*

OLD MAN. You can't get me off your back, young man. I'm here to stay.

SINBAD THE SAILOR. Get off... *(He tries several different ways to pry the OLD MAN, to spin him around, to lift him off, but none of the ways seem to work. Nothing he can do will get the OLD MAN off.)* I can't get you off my back.

OLD MAN. I told you.

SINBAD THE SAILOR. Forever?

OLD MAN. You'll become very attached to me.

SINBAD THE SAILOR *(suddenly noticing)*. You smell bad.

OLD MAN. You'll grow fond of that smell. Every time you smell it, you will think of me. And whenever you think of me, I'll be here.

SINBAD THE SAILOR. At least we can go to Baghdad. Perhaps I can get you removed there.

OLD MAN. I'm afraid not. But you'll get used to me. *(Pause.)* I'm hungry.

SINBAD THE SAILOR. Hungry? What do you eat?

OLD MAN. Coconuts.

SINBAD THE SAILOR. Ah, we were supposed to go to the Indies and trade for coconuts.

OLD MAN. That's where you are, young man. The Indies. And I can teach you how to get the coconuts. Go that way. To the Mountain of Apes. *(He points, SINBAD goes that direction.)* Now that way.

(This keeps going as OLD MAN leads SINBAD around. Two APES enter and rearrange the set into the Land of Palm Trees. They also drop a few "pebbles" to the ground. They are holding "palm trees" with detachable coconuts. SINBAD and OLD MAN notice the APES, high up in the coconut trees.)

SINBAD THE SAILOR. Apes.

OLD MAN. Yes. Now pick up a pebble. *(SINBAD does.)* And throw it at the Apes.

SINBAD THE SAILOR. But they've done nothing to me.

OLD MAN. You don't need to hit them. Just throw it at them.

SINBAD THE SAILOR. Whatever you say.

(He throws a pebble. The APES get mad and look around, pull coconuts down and throw them at SINBAD, clearly imitating him.)

OLD MAN. You see.

SINBAD THE SAILOR *(picks up coconuts, then another pebble)*. I see. *(He throws another pebble. APES throw coconuts back.)* They are very smart.

OLD MAN. They're not so smart. They just imitate what you do.

SINBAD THE SAILOR. Maybe they aren't so smart. But I am.

(He throws another pebble, hitting one APE squarely in the head, then he quickly turns and backs up to the tree. The APE grabs a coconut and kaboshes the OLD MAN on the head. The OLD MAN goes flying off SINBAD's shoulders, never to be seen again.)

OLD MAN. Oooouch. I'm faaaaaallllling!

SINBAD THE SAILOR *(takes the coconuts and waves at the APES)*. Thanks for the coconuts, Apes!

(The APES lumber off, taking the OLD MAN with them. SINBAD rearranges the set for the "China," a taller mountain with the "sun" behind it.)

SINBAD THE SAILOR. So there I was. Sinbad the Merchant. I traded the coconuts for passage back to Baghdad and— *(Rhythmically.) That* is the *story* of my *(beat)* fifth *voyage. (Speaks.)* Rich again, I had everything I needed. But still I wasn't content. When I reached the age of fifty-seven, I bought my own ship and returned to sea. *(Rhythmically.) This* is the *story* of my *(beat)* sixth *voyage*!

(#12: TRAVEL WITH TREASURE TAG, 6TH VOYAGE)

SINBAD THE SAILOR *(spoken).* I was determined to sail to China. *(SINBAD sails the ship himself. He sings as he goes.)*

I'm not content, I can't stand still.
I don't know that I ever will.
My restless soul draws me to roam,
The seven seas I call my home.

SINBAD THE SAILOR *("docks" the ship).* Hmm, no shipwreck, no monsters. Perhaps *I* wasn't the unlucky one.

(A beautiful WOMAN enters, seemingly cloaked in a white shroud. Very exotic, slow, beautiful music swells.)

WOMAN WITH WINGS. You. Man from far away. Who are you?

SINBAD THE SAILOR. Sinbad the Merchant. I've come
to trade.

WOMAN WITH WINGS. You've come to see the truth.
You've come to learn. You've come to fly with me to
the sun.

SINBAD THE SAILOR. No one can fly to the sun.

WOMAN WITH WINGS. I can, with these wings. *(She
spreads the shroud out into a huge, beautiful set of
wings that go out at least five feet from her body each
direction.)*

SINBAD THE SAILOR. Don't be ridiculous.

WOMAN WITH WINGS. But you sail across the seas,
with wings on your boat.

SINBAD THE SAILOR. I suppose.

WOMAN WITH WINGS. Then why do you not suppose I
can sail through the sky, with wings on my arms.

SINBAD THE SAILOR. Perhaps you could. But I've never
seen anything like it—

WOMAN WITH WINGS. Oh, yes, you have. You've seen
the Rukh.

SINBAD THE SAILOR. I've flown with the Rukh. Attached to the Ruhk, by rope or by snake.

WOMAN WITH WINGS. You are a man who has hung by
a thread from the claw of the Rukh, and yet you are too
afraid to fly with me to the sun?

SINBAD THE SAILOR. I'm not afraid. I'm Sinbad, and
I've never turned away from danger.

WOMAN WITH WINGS *(reaches back and lifts up a
smaller set of wings for SINBAD)*. Then take these
wings, Sinbad, and fly with me to the sun.

SINBAD THE SAILOR. It just doesn't seem right. But I'll accept your challenge. *(He puts the wings on and spreads them.)*

(A beautiful sun rises high in the sky.)

WOMAN WITH WINGS. The sun over China is beautiful, you see. Shiny like gold. If we fly there, we can collect the gold in your bag. Then we will have all wealth, all truth, and all beauty. Fly with me.

(They begin a slow pattern of sweeping figure eights about the stage as the music builds and swells.)

SINBAD THE SAILOR. The sun is not a treasure—we can't possess it. We shall die.

WOMAN WITH WINGS. Nonsense. If you believe, you can do anything. The sun is mine to have, and yours. Believe with me and fly with me.

(WOMAN continues flying dance, SINBAD following. Lights get brighter and brighter as they "fly" higher and higher.)

SINBAD THE SAILOR. Please, no closer. We'll be killed. The sun is so hot!

WOMAN WITH WINGS. Fly with me, fly!

SINBAD THE SAILOR. Turn back! You are too close to the face of the sun, too close!

WOMAN WITH WINGS. Fly! Fly!

(Music soars and suddenly there is a great flash of light and sound as the WOMAN screams, swirling and crumbling to the ground and offstage.)

SINBAD THE SAILOR. No! No, I'm turning back!

(SINBAD's wings begin to crumble as he struggles to turn and lands on the ground. Lights change and the music begins a rich deep sweeping jungle sound. GRANDFATHER ELEPHANT walks on and past SIN-BAD.)

SINBAD THE SAILOR. Great feats of Allah, what strange beast is this? Where am I?

(As the ELEPHANT leaves, a RAJAH in turban with a huge sword appears and stands over SINBAD.)

RAJAH. You are in India, friend. I am the Rajah and I saw you come from the sky.

SINBAD THE SAILOR. Where is the Woman with Wings?

RAJAH. I saw only you. Where are you from?

SINBAD THE SAILOR. Baghdad, Your Majesty, where the mighty Sultan rules.

RAJAH. Ah, and he sent you to me, as an ambassador.

SINBAD THE SAILOR. Actually ...

RAJAH. Do not speak anymore. Here, take this treasure to your Sultan and tell him I have more. *(Gives SINBAD treasure and a turban. SINBAD puts it on.)* Bring back word from him. Perhaps our nations can be friends. Go, Sinbad the Ambassador.

SINBAD THE SAILOR. Yes, Your Majesty.

(RAJAH leaves. SINBAD sets up The Elephant's Grave-yard as he whispers in rhythm.)

(#13: SINBAD CHANT, 5TH-7TH VOYAGES)

SINBAD THE SAILOR. That was the *story* of my *(beat)* sixth *voyage*! and ...

(See #13: SINBAD CHANT, 5TH-7TH VOYAGES)

SINBAD THE SAILOR. *This* is the *story* of my *(beat)* last *voyage*! *(Spoken.)* Ten years it took me to go back and forth from India to Baghdad, so by the time I returned I was sixty-seven years old.

(RAJAH enters, a bow and arrows in hand.)

SINBAD THE SAILOR. Your Majesty, Rajah, my Sultan sends you greetings and says that I am to ask for alliance between our countries.

RAJAH. If we are to have alliance, I must have wealth as great as that of Persia.

SINBAD THE SAILOR. We will give you all you desire.

RAJAH. No. I would have the wealth I need if I could claim enough of the elephants. Take this bow and hunt the elephants. *(Gives SINBAD the bow and arrows.)* When you shoot the elephants, bring me the ivory tusks. I need as many tusks as blades of grass in the fields.

SINBAD THE SAILOR. I said that my master, the Sultan, would give you wealth.

RAJAH. I cannot accept his gifts if I have nothing to give in return. Kill the elephant. Bring me the tusks and we will talk of peace.

SINBAD THE SAILOR. But I don't wish to kill the elephants. I am an old man.

RAJAH *(lifting the sword high over SINBAD's head, threatening him)*. And you will be a dead man if you refuse me. An ambassador is at the whim of the King, the Sultan, the Rajah. Do as I say. If you want peace between our countries, do as I say.

SINBAD THE SAILOR. Yes, Rajah.

(SINBAD lifts bow. RAJAH stands at a distance. SINBAD turns and sees "small cutout ELEPHANTS" which appear over The Elephant's Graveyard. They are built like "flip targets." SINBAD shoots an arrow and an elephant falls.)

RAJAH. Another. *(SINBAD shoots again.)* Another. *(SINBAD shoots again.)* Another.

(RAJAH leaves. SINBAD starts to shoot again, but GRANDFATHER ELEPHANT enters slowly. GRANDFATHER ELEPHANT is very big and walks up to SINBAD, raises his trunk, trumpets. SINBAD gets ready to shoot, then drops the bow and cowers.)

SINBAD THE SAILOR. Go ahead, Grandfather Elephant. I deserve to die.

GRANDFATHER ELEPHANT *(in a huge voice)*. Sinbad the Sailor.

SINBAD THE SAILOR. Yes?

GRANDFATHER ELEPHANT. Come with me. I will show you what you need to see.

(SINBAD walks behind GRANDFATHER ELEPHANT, who leads him to The Elephant's Graveyard. SINBAD moves a set piece and reveals the huge skull of an elephant surrounded by many tusks and bones.)

SINBAD THE SAILOR. The Elephant's Graveyard. There are tusks all over.

GRANDFATHER ELEPHANT. These you shall have. Not my children.

SINBAD THE SAILOR. Yes, Grandfather Elephant.

(GRANDFATHER ELEPHANT leaves. SINBAD leans down and picks up two tusks, holds them majestically in the air. Music swells, a victory. RAJAH enters again.)

SINBAD THE SAILOR. Rajah. I have found The Elephant's Graveyard. You need not hunt anymore and all the ivory you wish shall be yours.

RAJAH. Well done, Sinbad. There shall be peace between our countries.

(He gives SINBAD more treasure, then bows and exits. PORTER enters as SINBAD chants, rhythmically.)

(#14: SINBAD CHANT, ACCOMPANIMENT)

SINBAD THE SAILOR. *That* is the *story* of my *(beat)* seventh *voyage. (PORTER smiles as SINBAD talks.)* And so, my friend, Sinbad the Porter, my namesake, now you know my story. How I came to be so wealthy and so powerful at the age of seventy-seven.

(As he talks, MERCHANT and FIRST MATE enter with boat, waiting for SINBAD THE PORTER to join them.)

SINBAD THE PORTER. I've listened to your stories, Sinbad the Horseman, Sinbad the Adventurer, Sinbad the Hero, Sinbad the Husband, Sinbad the Merchant, Sinbad the Ambassador, Sinbad the Sailor, and I thank you for seven meals and seven bags of gold. But now, it is my turn. Today, I will buy trade goods and set sail and...

(PORTER steps into the boat, holding the mast, just as SINBAD THE SAILOR has been doing, then he chants rhythmically.)

(Repeat #14)

SINBAD THE PORTER. *This* is the *story* of my *(beat)* first *voyage*!

(Blackout. REFRAIN of opening song as they all come out and bow.)

END OF PLAY

NOTES ON THE SET:

Several examples of "block building the set."

ISLAND OF THE SEA MONSTER

For this it is possible to lay the two ramps flat each rising to center stage, with a three foot gap between them. This gap is bridged by a plank. The Sea Monster enters, and slides under the plank, tentacles sticking out forward. When Sinbad is on the Island, he reaches down and pulls the hair of the monster.

ISLAND OF THE GIANT RUKH AND DIAMONDS

For this, the two ramps are set on their wide end, so they peak up and look like three foot tall mountains, the triangle of their construction facing the audience. There is a small gap between them, and they are angled so an actor can hide behind them. This actor pushes the snakes through the gap, then sets up and manipulates the baby Rukh puppet. This actor can also place additional diamonds and treasure on the side of the mountain.

ISLAND OF THE OLD MAN

Again, the ramps can be set up leading to each other, but with no top to them, so the gap between represents the stream the old man wishes to cross.

ISLAND OF THE APES

The two triangles stand up again, spaced apart so each ape can stand behind it, planting his palm tree.

All of the above are suggestions. The important thing is to create a very versatile and flexible unit set that allows for many different locations to be created by the actors at "play."

PUPPETRY and COSTUMES:

The Seven Voyages of Sinbad the Sailor is intended to be "transformational" theatre; the sets and costumes suggested and brought into play rather than specifically detailed. Period and culturally specific base costumes may be worn by the actors at all times with costume pieces added as needed. Props and puppets may add to the flavor of the time period and genre. Puppets should be worn "over" the base costume—completely covering the body in the case of the ISLAND MONSTER, or just an extension of the upper body in the case of the RUKH. The OLD MAN can be a handheld marionette in the Japanese style, with the actor wearing a black shirt and speaking for the puppet, but in plain sight of the audience. GRANDFATHER ELEPHANT should be a complete "body" puppet with stilts attached to the hands to provide front legs for the elephant. The play requires crystal-clear characterization from the actors surrounding SINBAD so that each is distinct. SINBAD himself should be consistent and yet age through the play.

DIRECTOR'S NOTES

DIRECTOR'S NOTES

DIRECTOR'S NOTES

DIRECTOR'S NOTES

DIRECTOR'S NOTES

DIRECTOR'S NOTES